Epiphany Echoes

Aishwarya Padmanabhan

BookLeaf
Publishing

India | USA | UK

Made with ❤ on the BookLeaf Publishing Platform
www.bookleafpub.in
www.bookleafpub.com

Dedication

Preface

This book is about my journey through my twenties. It's a collection of memories, feelings, and moments that shaped who I am. These pages hold stories about my family and friends . They capture my experiences, the challenges I faced, and the friendships that helped me through tough times.

I've written these poems to remember where I've been and how far I've come. Some memories are happy, some are challenging, but all of them are true. This is my way of looking back and seeing my own strength—how I survived, learned, and grew.

These aren't just poems. They're pieces of my life—moments of doubt, bursts of joy, and everything in between. It's a reminder to myself of how much I've overcome, how much I've learned, and how much I've become.

This is my story. Raw. Real. Mine.

Acknowledgements

1. My Patriarch

Growing up ,I thought it the norm
Mom and Dad , roles never deformed

Chores shared , no gender in sight
A household of balance , always so right

It wasn't until much later I'd learn
that our upbringing was exception and not the norm

For most , a difference would still remain ,
sons and daughter unequal domains

But my parents , the showed in the ways,
No boundaries of gender to sway.

Opportunities equal, love without bounds,
A grateful heart , this truth resounds

2. The Story My Amma Told

Amma shared a tale when I was small,
About a wise man, kind and tall.

Each evening as he walked his way,
A family would warmly say:
"Please join us for our dinner sage!"
This went on day by day , with age.

He'd smile and thank them with his heart,
But choose to kindly stay apart.

When death drew near , he told his son,
"Remember what these folks have done.
They'll ask you too to share their meal-
This gift of love is true and real."

The son rushed in with eager joy,
Like someone with a brand new toy.
Too quick to take what they would give,
Not knowing how to let love live.

Soon they stopped asking him to come,
And Amma would say with wisdom warm:
"Some bonds are like a gentle stream,
Best kept flowing, like a dream."

3. Soul Compass

When things feel hard and tears might fall,
I know you hear my quiet call,

My heart feels light when I just say
" Please help me find my way today "

Like sunshine warm upon my face,
Your love fills every empty space.

And when I fear I might lose ground
You help me turn my life around

So ill keep walking , knowing you're there
My heart held safely in your loving care

For faith lights up the road I cannot see,
And guides me to the best that I can be .

4. Parting Ways

Like travelers on a moving trains,
Our friendship passed ,
then slipped away again

I thought you'd be my shield ,my steady ground
But life's a journey where We're just passing round

Some board and leave at their appointed stop
No permanence ,Just moments that just drop

We're passengers, brief sparks along the way
Connected briefly ,then we fade away

5. I Got My Girls !

Through mascara tears and midnight calls,
You've held my hand through all my falls.

No judgement in your gentle eyes,
Just tissues ,truth and warm replies.

We share our dreams over coffee cups
Celebrating each others way up.

You fix my crown without a word,
Make sure my voice is always heard.

In you I found my chosen clan,
Sisters who help me understand

That strength lie not in standing tall,
But having friends who catch your fall

Like angels sent from stars above
You wrap me in your endless love

In this world of changing parts
You're home forever in my heart

6. Mixed Balance

Some days bring sunshine ,
And some days bring rain,
Success and stress both joy and pain.

Good news come with morning light ,
But worries made my chest feel tight.

Each victory seemed to bring along ,
A challenge testing if I'm strong.

Yet looking back , I clearly see,
The good outweighed what troubled me.

Its all in how we choose to look ,
At stories in life's daily book.

So now I choose to count the light ,
And let the shadows fade from sight.

7. Wake Me Up When September Ends

My pillow's wet with midnight tears,
As September whispers in my ears.
I don't know why I feel this way,
Just want to hide and sleep all day.

Amma keeps asking "Are you okay molu ?"
But words are hard for me to say.
The mirror shows my puffy eyes,
As clouds fill up these autumn skies.

Sometimes I just stare at walls,
While time so slowly crawls.
My phone keeps ringing, I don't pick up,
Feels like I've spilled my happiness cup.

Each morning brings the same old fight,
To find a tiny spark of light.
My heart feels heavy in my chest,
As I fail another simple test.

I keep on pushing, day by day,
Though I don't know if I'm okay.
September feels so awfully long,
Like a sad and endless song.

Just wake me when this month has passed,
When these gray clouds won't last.
Till then I'll wrap myself in blue,
And dream of skies once bright and new.

8. Thirty's Wisdom

My Twenties rushed like wild winds
Through days of endless start and ends
Always running, always bold
Chasing stories left untold

Time felt short and dreams felt big
Racing forward, branch and twig
Till wisdom whispered , soft and sweet:
"Slow down , dear heart, find your beat"

Now as thirty gently nears
Gone are all those rushing fears
Drama fades like morning mist
Peace finds me- I'm glad I missed

All those fights that seemed so key
Now I know what sets me free
walking down my chosen road
Carrying wisdom's gentle load

At last I dance to my own song
Here's where I've belonged all along

12

9. 'Sorted' , Hmmm..."Nah !"

Sometimes I watch the world go by,
See others soar while I still try,
Their paths seem clear as morning light,
While mine's a puzzle in the night.
But wisdom comes in gentle waves,
Teaching me that everyone craves
The same sweet peace I'm searching for
We're all just learning, evermore.
Behind each smile that seems so sure,
Behind each step that looks secure,
Are countless moments just like mine:
Of doubt, of growth, of redesign.
Some climb mountains, some walk plains,
Some dance in sun, some walk through rains,
But none have reached their final page
We're all still writing on life's stage.
Each stumble teaches how to dance,
Each wrong turn brings another chance,
Each doubt that makes my heart feel small
Reminds me we're still growing tall.

So let your shoulders drop their weight,
Your journey's neither soon nor late,
You're exactly where you need to be
Perfect in your progress, wild and free.
For in this vast and winding show,
There's just one truth we need to know:
We're all works in progress divine,
Taking one step at a time.

10. Of Course! For The Love Of True Living

When doubts creep in and questions rise
About the path before my eyes,
I sometimes wonder, "Why this way?"
"What fruit will bloom from seeds today?"

But the old friend- wisdom, whispers: "Don't you see?
The joy's in what makes your heart free.
Some choose to drift in idle seas,
While others chase what makes them breathe."

The beauty lies in choosing right
Not for rewards that shine so bright,
But for the warmth it brings your soul,
For how it makes your being whole.

So paint or write or build or sing,
Not for the praise your art might bring,
But for the peace it plants within
That's where true living does begin.

11. The Simple Ask

Each morning at my desk I sat,
Content, but knew there could be that

Little spark of something more ,
Waiting just beyond the door .

One day I gathered up my might ,
Asked my boss to shine more bright .

No mountains moved, no storms did break,
Just simple words I had to make.

Now here I am with tasks anew,
Smiling at what words can do .

Sometimes all it takes to grow,
Is just to let someone else know
The greatest change can start so small,
With just one voice , just one call

12. When Life says "Yeah, Right!"

I made my plans all neat and clean,
Like drawing stars I'd never seen.
"I've got this now!" I said with joy ,
Like a kid who got her favorite toy.

The door I knocked on opened wide,
I walked in with a spring of pride.
"Just watch me now, I'll show you all!"
(That's usually when we trip and fall)

The thing I wanted ,wrapped so nice,
Came with a funny little slice
Of something that I didn't pick
Life's way of playing its small trick!

So now i laugh when things go right,
And keep my wishes soft and light
Because when I say "Now I know!"
Life smiles and whispers, " Wait and see though..."

13. Error 404 : Chill Not Found

My mind runs everyday
Thinking of things that might go wrong.
Though people say , "It's all okay,"
These worries still tag along

I plan and plan all day long
About all the things that might go wrong
By evening ,when the day is done
I see things all done and i worried for none

Part of me still can't let go,
Of all these "what-ifs" in my head.
Even when things smoothly flow,
I fill my head with so much dread.

It's funny how life teaches me,
That most fears don't come true at all.
Maybe someday I will see,
That I don't need to fear the fall.

Till then .I'll take it day by day
Learning slowly - that's okay

14. My Quiet Sunflower

That first day , you peeked around your desk,
Eyes bright with joy to see me there,
Another woman joining the quest,
Your welcome showed how much you care.

You shared the little things with me ,
Coffee breaks and building tours,
Your kindness flowed so naturally,
Opening all the hidden doors.

In shared cabs , through tears and smiles ,
We built a friendship pure and true,
No questions asked , just understanding,
Silent support between us two.

You're more than just a colleague now,
A friend who makes work feel like home,
Thankyou for your gentle heart,
For making sure I'm not alone.

15. A Vijayan Love Letter

Like Dasan's wild ,ridiculous schemes,
I burst through life with maximum noise.
You roll your eyes at my crazy dreams,
My calm Vijayan, my friendship's true voice.
Four months of silence- drama supreme!
Then Sunday's "Hello" broke everything through.
I cried ,I laughed ,I shared everything,
You listened. And I must say That's so you!.
No fancy words, no dramatic pause,
You catch me when my world goes for spins.
Like our Nadodikakattu heroes know:
True friendship starts where the chaos begins.
They say time has its own sweet way ,
Of keeping real friends close to heart
So here's to us -My Vijaya , my friend , my personal guide,
Who puts up with my dramatic tide

16. Chronic Quitter

"She's a chronic Quitter !" *Amma's astrologer declared*
(As if my stars had somehow misbehaved and erred)
Two years at my first job,then I walked away
Another position- brief hello,quick goodbye,wouldn't stay

Calligraphy class? Left my pens behind
Dancing and singing? Changed my mind
Four books a month I used to read
Till I asked myself,"Is this what I actually need?"

Some friendships too, I let them go
When they brought more dark circles than skin glow
People whispered , shook their heads with shame
"There she goes again"-- my quitter's fame

But here's what wisdom has to say:
Your past shouldn't chain your today
"Think of all you've invested here!"
They plead , as if time makes chains more dear

That Job i "quit" ? Lead to better things
Those unread books ? Found ones that made to my soul
The friendships lost? Made room for true ones to start
Sometimes quitting is the **wisest art**

It's not giving up- its choosing more
It's knowing what's worth fighting for
It's saying "yes" to your own worth
Even when doubt your course

So call me a Quitter if you must
But I've learned to deeply trust
That walking away can set you free
To become who you're meant to be

17. Let Them Breathe

Two babies born , both pure and new,
Both hearts beat strong and true .

But one they Praise "So fair, so bright!",
While one brings frown:"A bit too dark..."

Why must we judge these tiny souls
Before they've lived a day ?

Each child deserves the same warm love
No matter what their colors say

18. Different Routes Home

My brother walks with quiet grace,
Achieving dreams at his own pace.
Excellence in all he chose to do,
His path straight and purpose true.

While I took the louder route,
Making headlines everyday !
My results would make such news
The neighbours knew all my ups and downs.

He found his path right on time ,
While I'm still working on mine .
Studies took me extra years,
But brought me joy and calmed my fears.

We're different stars in the same sky,
Each shining bright in our own time.
I'm proud of both our stories true,
Each perfect in our own route too .

19. The Daily Reset

Bad days hit me pretty hard,
Leave me feeling tired and scarred,
Then I found this simple key—
Each reset can set me free.

Whether I laugh or if I cry,
Hours tick and moments fly,
Twenty-four, then start anew,
Like the morning's fresh-dropped dew.

Time won't pause to ease my pain,
But brings reset with dawn again,
Good or bad, each day must end,
Like a game that lets me mend.

When the clock strikes twelve at night,
Everything resets just right,
Yesterday just fades away,
As I load another day.

So when life feels much too rough,
And my heart's had quite enough,
I remember what is true:
Each reset brings something new.

One day ends, another loads,
Clearing all the heavy roads,
Teaching me with every night:
Tomorrow's screen might be bright.

Like a game that starts again,
Wiping clean both joy and pain,
And no matter what life brings,
Every reset gives me wings.

So I'll take it reset by reset,
Making peace with what I get,
Finding strength in what I know:
Each new start helps me to grow.

20. Warm Hugs

In silence we build our walls so high ,
Keeping thoughts locked deep inside .

Each struggling with our own dark night ,
While thinking other just don't get our fight .

You carry burdens I cannot see,
Just as yours remain unknown to me .

We walk these path,so close yet far,
Each bearing weight beneath our scars.

But when we dare to break these walls,
When pride and fear finally falls,

I see the storms you're walking through,
Mirror the ones I'm battling too

Sometimes words aren't what we need,
Just arms that hold us while we breathe.

In that embrace, we both can find,
The peace that heals our weary minds.

Know that I'm here , through storm and sun,
Two hearts beating, yet bound as one .

www.ingramcontent.com/pod-product-compliance
Lightning Source LLC
LaVergne TN
LVHW010022200726
843495LV00015B/1886